Born to Do This

"Wow! This devotional is incredible—I found myself reading the prayers one after the other for many days in a row. Joan is such an inspirational spiritual example: a simple girl who willed God's will and became a hero and a saint. As you read a bit of her story every day, you will find encouragement to face the challenges of your day, too."

Kristyn L. Brown
Photographer and creator of The Saints Project

"From the life of an extraordinary saint, we can learn lessons for ordinary life. This book helps us see the adventure we're living every day—in temptations, in spiritual warfare, and in the company of angels. St. Joan teaches us to listen in our prayer and open our eyes to the world as it really is."

Mike Aquilina
Author and editor of the Reclaiming Catholic History series

Born to Do This

GREAT SPIRITUAL TEACHERS

30 DAYS WITH

Joan of Arc

Edited by Jaymie Stuart Wolfe

Ave Maria Press AVE Notre Dame, Indiana

Series editor: John Kirvan

Founded in 1865, Ave Maria Press is a ministry of the United States Province of Holy Cross.

www.avemariapress.com

Paperback: ISBN-13 978-1-64680-360-6

E-book: ISBN-13 978-1-64680-361-3

Cover art of Joan of Arc © Iryna Kirepko, www.etsy.com/shop/CreativeIconsByIrina.

Cover and text design by Katherine Robinson Coleman.

Printed and bound in the United States of America.

Contents

Timeline

Note: The Gregorian calendar was created in 1582, more than 150 years after the death of Joan of Arc. Prior to its universal adoption (most recently England and its territories in 1752), March 25 was the first day of the calendar year. Because of this, we still encounter discrepancies in the year given for historical events that occurred before March 25 in any given year. The years used here are given according to the way we currently reckon time.

1412	Joan of Arc born in Domrémy
1424	Summer: Joan's first encounter with her voices
1428	October 12: The English begin the siege of Orléans
1429	February: Joan leaves home and travels to Vaucouleurs to ask for an escort to the king
	March 4: Joan arrives at Chinon and meets Charles VII
	March–April: Joan is examined extensively by theologians at Poitiers
	April 29: Joan arrives at Orléans

	May 8: Victory at Orléans; the siege is lifted and the English withdraw
	July 17: Coronation of Charles VII as king of France at Rheims Cathedral; numerous military campaigns follow by which cities are brought under Charles's rule
	September 8: Joan is defeated in Paris
	November 24: Joan is defeated in La Charité
1430	May 23: Joan is captured by Burgundian forces at Compiègne
	December 23: Joan arrives at Rouen and is imprisoned
1431	January 9: Preparatory heresy trial begins
	February 21: Joan's first appearance in court
	March 26: Ordinary Trial begins
	May 19: University of Paris condemns Joan
	May 23: Formal charges against Joan
	May 24: Joan abjures
	May 28: Joan withdraws her abjuration

May 29: Joan is handed over to civil authorities

May 30: Joan is burned at the stake as a relapsed heretic

December 16: Henry VI, King of England, is crowned King of France in Paris

Circa 1435 City of Orléans begins annual parade honoring Joan's raising the siege

1436 April 13: Charles VII reclaims Paris

1440 Charles, Duke of Orléans, is released by the English

1449 France reclaims the city of Rouen under Charles VII

Joan's mother and brothers petition Pope Nicholas V to reopen her case

1450 Charles VII initiates an investigation of the original trial

1452 Cardinal Guillaume d'Estouteville continues investigation

1455 Pope Callixtus III authorizes a formal retrial

1455–1456	Retrial conducted by Jean Bréhal, inquisitor general of France
1456	July 7: Pope issues a Decree of Nullification of the original trial verdict
1869	Pope Pius IX receives a petition for Joan's canonization
1894	Pope Leo XIII opens Joan's cause for canonization
1904	January 6: Decree of Joan's Heroic Virtue issued
	January 8: Joan of Arc declared Venerable by Pope St. Pius X
1909	April 18: Pope St. Pius X beatifies Joan
1920	May 16: Pope Benedict XV canonizes Joan of Arc

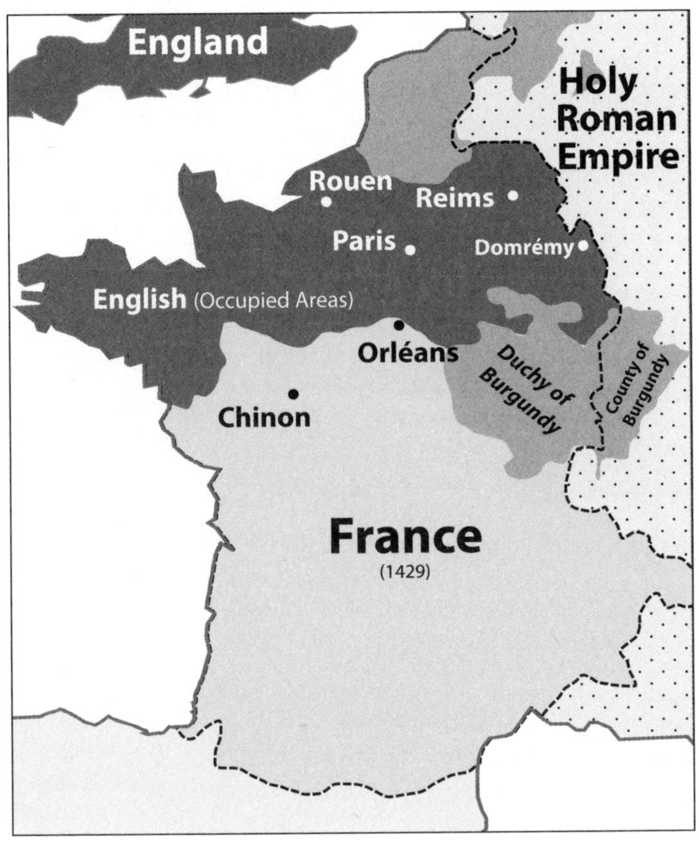
England
Holy
Roman
Empire
Rouen
Reims
Paris
Domrémy
English (Occupied Areas)
Orléans
Duchy of
Burgundy
County of
Burgundy
Chinon
France
(1429)

WHO IS
Joan of Arc?

Joan was born in 1412, in a small village, Domrémy, in northeastern France during the Hundred Years' War. Joan grew up on a successful family farm along with three brothers and one sister. She was not formally educated and could neither read nor write. By all accounts, Joan was a religious child; she began hearing what she called her "voices" when she was in her thirteenth year, during the summer of 1424.

Joan was skilled in spinning and sewing but was never trained to use a sword or ride a horse. Nevertheless, she led an army of French men against English occupying forces at the age of seventeen. Her numerous military victories—especially at Orléans—made it possible for the *dauphin*, the French heir to the throne, to be crowned Charles VII, King of France. Joan kept the English from conquering France entirely and turned the tide of the Hundred Years' War. As a result, the sovereignty of France was preserved, and English forces eventually returned home in defeat.

Despite her many accomplishments, however, Joan's life did not end in accolade. Both the English and their numerous French collaborators sought to discredit the legitimacy of Charles VII. These political maneuvers resulted in Joan's arrest, trial, and ultimately her execution. Our heroine was burned alive at the stake in Rouen on May 30, 1431. She was nineteen.

Joan of Arc is a lot like a Rorschach inkblot test: people tend to see in her whatever they want to see. To some, Joan is a typical medieval peasant girl. To others, she is a young radical, centuries ahead of her time. This is possible because our spiritual teacher was a young woman of many paradoxes.

- Joan was a young, illiterate girl, yet she issued ultimatums to English commanders and even their king and spoke about theological matters with both knowledge and eloquence at her trial.
- She was armed with the legendary sword of the acclaimed Charles Martel but preferred her banner to the sword and never killed anyone in battle.
- Joan dressed in men's clothing, but she did so as a practical matter and to guard her chastity.
- She exercised brilliant strategic and tactical military leadership but also led her men in virtue. Joan expelled prostitutes, required her soldiers to make confessions and attend Mass, and expected them to stop swearing and refrain from looting civilians.
- Joan was unrelenting against the enemies of France, yet she was seen weeping over the bodies of dead English soldiers because they had not been given an opportunity to receive absolution beforehand.

Her men loved her. Her enemies envied her.

Joan was inspiring, but she was also controversial. Consequently, she suffered persecution, as have many mystics before her and since. She was suspected of witchcraft, heresy, mental illness, and rejecting the limitations and proper station of her sex. Everything that could be used against her was—and mercilessly. Deprived of her rights under both civil and canon law, she was not merely imprisoned but tortured.

We know these things because the transcripts of Joan of Arc's canonical trials—her condemnation as well as the inquiries and nullification, or retrial, held twenty-five years after her death—are preserved. They constitute a rich source of information about Joan and her contemporaries, as well as a window into European life at the end of the Middle Ages. We know Joan's story largely because of these documents. Because both public and private interrogations were officially recorded, we can hear Joan speak for herself. And while we will also listen to the eyewitness testimony of some who knew her, listening to Joan is the purpose of this book. To that end, statements attributed to various people—most especially to Joan herself—have been presented here in the first person. Where historical context for her words is needed, it has been provided briefly as a note.

Joan of Arc has been celebrated as a national hero since her first victory in 1429. The city of Orléans, France, has held an annual parade in her honor since 1435, less than five years after her death. This tradition has continued, with few interruptions, for nearly six hundred years. Joan was officially vindicated and declared a martyr by the Church in 1456. At the same time, Pierre Cauchon, the corrupt bishop who presided over her show trial and handed her over for execution, was posthumously excommunicated. But it took nearly five centuries for Joan's cause for canonization to make much progress. The heroic degree of Joan's Christian virtues was not officially recognized until Pope Leo XIII declared her Venerable in 1894. She was beatified by Pope St. Pius X in 1909 and canonized by Pope Benedict XV in 1920, shortly after the end of the First World War.

Joan of Arc's brief life can be envisioned in three acts: Mysticism, Mission, and Martyrdom. Over the next thirty days, we will accompany her in those three aspects of her story—and invite her to accompany us with the hope that the courageous faith we admire in her will become our own.

HOW TO
Use This Book

The books in the Great Spiritual Teachers series provide an introduction to the spiritual insights and wisdom of some of history's most extraordinary saints. Through these pages, you're invited to a place beyond mere reading, into an experience of daily prayer and meditation. You'll be accompanied by a spiritual teacher whose wisdom will awaken, enrich, and empower your walk with the Lord.

In other words, these books take you on a spiritual journey.

We have some suggestions for how you can make the most of this journey. But keep in mind that these books are meant to help you experience the freedom and joy of communing with God in prayer. The daily format is there to help—but don't hesitate to go at your own pace or take your own route! Repeat a day as often as you like, or skip a day if the reading isn't resonating with where you are in your journey. The goal is to hear the voice of God through the words of the saints.

However you choose to use this book, it's helpful to understand the thinking behind the format used for each day. We've chosen to follow the suggestion of the classic book on spirituality *The Cloud of Unknowing*, which describes a three-part movement of *reading*, *reflecting*, and *praying*: "These three are so linked together that there can be no profitable reflection without first reading or hearing. Nor will beginners or even the spiritually adept come to true prayer without first taking time to reflect on what they have heard or read."

Throughout these thirty days you'll follow in the footsteps of this long-standing tradition. Each day starts with a section called "My Day Begins," in which you'll find a passage quoted or adapted from a great spiritual teacher. This is followed by "All Through the Day," which provides a short, memorable phrase (drawn from or based on the reading) that you can carry with you throughout the day, enabling you to reflect and meditate on a key truth, question, or insight. In the final section, "My Day Is Ending," you're encouraged to find a quiet place to go to the Lord in prayer, drawing on that day's reading as you lift up your petitions and praises to him.

My Day Begins

One of the best ways you can begin your day is to put yourself in the company of a great spiritual teacher.

The selected passages are short—just a few hundred words. But they are powerful! They've been chosen specifically for their ability to provide spiritual focus for your day and to remind you that you are a spiritual being, intended for relationship and intimacy with God.

These morning readings don't just put you in the presence of a spiritual teacher who can accompany you on your journey—they are also designed to invite you into God's presence so you can start your day in conversation with him.

If you find that you don't fully understand the reading, don't be discouraged! Understanding may come with time, meditation, and further prayer. For now, focus on your heart's response. Tell the Lord about the questions you have, and ask him for wisdom and insight.

It's also helpful to read *slowly*. We've divided the passages into sense lines to help you do just that. Instead of rushing through the reading, savor each word. Pay attention to which phrases or images resonate in your heart. Make room for God to speak. In short, read prayerfully. Each day's opening reading is meant to foster attentiveness to God and an attitude of readiness to hear what he wants to say to you.

All Through the Day

After the day's reading you'll find a single sentence, a meditation that you can reflect on throughout your day. As you move forward with the busyness of everyday life, return to this reflection as often as you can. Try writing it down on a card and placing it somewhere you'll see it frequently. Or copy it down in a journal or planner. Recite it in the little free moments between tasks and conversations.

This reflection shouldn't take you out of the day's responsibilities. Rather, it should serve as a gentle reminder of God's presence within the many activities and tasks that make up your day—and an expression of your desire to live in connection with him.

My Day Is Ending

No matter what your day has brought to you, there's great wisdom in reaching the end of it and turning everything over to God in prayer, intentionally setting your mind and heart on him, and listening for his voice.

If you find that it's not easy to let go of the events of the day, to find peace and closure and solace in God's presence, here are some suggestions to help you:

1. Find a quiet, distraction-free place that you can return to each evening.
2. Quiet your spirit. Sometimes this involves relaxing your body and letting go of physical tension. Try adopting a posture that reminds you that you are in God's presence: sit or kneel; fold your hands or lift them up—whatever works for you. Focus on breathing deeply and deliberately.
3. When you feel calm and at peace, focus on the evening prayer phrase by phrase. If you find yourself getting caught up in analyzing the words of the prayer, wrestling with the meaning of a phrase, or becoming distracted, don't worry! Just pause, breathe, and

begin again. Set aside all the distractions and worries that stand between you and God.

The time spent with the evening prayer doesn't need to be very long—just remember that it is a time of expressing complete trust and confidence in God, preparing yourself for a night of peaceful sleep. End the day as you began it, resting in his presence.

Some Other Ways to Use This Book

1. *Create your own reflections*. If the provided "All Through the Day" reflection doesn't resonate with you, or if you'd like to add to it, feel free to choose another phrase or image from the morning reading that caught your attention.
2. *Incorporate journaling into your spiritual journey*. Many find that journaling—through either copying out the provided reflections and prayers or writing your own—is an excellent way to slow down and focus, ensuring that your mind doesn't skip over important insights. Or you could use a journal to keep a record of your experiences on this thirty-day journey, such as the insights that had the biggest impact on your thinking or any daily changes you noticed in your heart or behavior.
3. *Look for contrasts*. Sometimes two readings or reflections might seem to stand in tension with each other.

Often, such tensions highlight areas for fruitful reflection. Write down the contrasting passages and any questions they raise. Meditate on them and pray about them—God may provide new illumination as you ponder!

4. *Form a small group.* You're not alone in seeking to deepen your spiritual life—so why not invite others to join you on your thirty-day journey with a great spiritual teacher? Try meeting weekly—whether over coffee or a shared meal—to discuss that week's readings, reflections, and prayers. Talk to each other about how God is working in your lives. Pray together.

We hope that you'll be richly blessed by the books in this series. As you intentionally fill your days with the words and wisdom of a great spiritual teacher, we pray that you'll be ushered daily into the divine presence, experiencing more deeply than ever the life-giving joy of intimacy with the God who loves you.

The Publisher

THIRTY DAYS WITH
Joan of Arc

DAY 1

My Day Begins

When she had taken the oath, Joan was questioned about her name and surname. "In my own country, I am called Jeannette, and after I came to France, I was called Jeanne. I know nothing about my surname. . . . I was born in the village of Domrémy."

Asked about the name of her father and mother, she replied, "My father's name is Jacques d'Arc, and my mother's Isabelle."

Asked where she was baptized, she replied, "It was in the church of Domrémy."

Asked how old she was, she replied, "I think nineteen. My mother taught me the Our Father, Hail Mary, and Creed. No one but my mother taught me my beliefs."

All Through the Day

Thank you, Lord, for all those who have brought faith to me.

My Day Is Ending

Lord God,
So much of who we are is given to us by others.
So much of what we believe, we inherit.
But ultimately, we belong to the One who made us. We are yours.
Help me to be grateful for all that has brought me to where I am,
for every grace I have received,
for every act that has benefited me, no matter how small,
for every word that has encouraged me, no matter how simple.
Keep me mindful of all the people who have touched my life,
especially those who revealed your presence to me in my childhood.
Show me how to nurture the seeds of faith others planted in my heart.
Help me to grow in my love for you.
Empower me to inspire those who come after me.
I do not know everything about myself,
but nothing is hidden from you.

In your perfect will, you have a purpose and a plan for my life.
Help me to receive and accept myself as your gift.
Make of me what you desire.
Give me the grace to embrace all the circumstances of my life,
to acknowledge who and what I am,
and who and what you are within me.
Amen.

DAY 2

My Day Begins

At the age of thirteen, I had a voice from God to help me and guide me. The first time I heard this voice, I was very much afraid. The voice came around noon, in the summer, in my father's garden. I had not fasted on the preceding day. I heard the voice on my right, in the direction of the church; I seldom hear it without a light appearing. The light came from the same side as the voice, and usually, there is a great light. When I came to France, I often heard the voice.

If I was in the woods, I easily heard the voices come to me. It seemed to me a worthy voice, and I believe it was sent from God. When I heard the voice a third time, I knew it was the voice of an angel. This voice always protected me well and I understood the voice well.

All Through the Day

Teach me how to recognize your voice, Lord.

My Day Is Ending

Loving and faithful God,
At times it is hard to hear your voice
because there are so many loud voices whirring around me
or there are too many competing voices within me.
All of them vie for my attention.
None of them speak peace.
Show me how to recognize your voice, Lord.
Give me the wisdom to distinguish your voice from all the others.
Help me to find silence in my soul.
Teach my heart to listen for you:
in the activities of daily life,
in unexpected encounters,
in times of sorrow and pain,
in moments of joy and comfort,
when I feel lonely, and when I am alone.
Help me to receive and understand your message to me.
Give me the grace to respond to your word
with all you have given me,
with all I have been,
with all I am,
and with all I hope to be.

Give me the courage to speak with a voice
that echoes with your truth,
announces your presence,
and inspires your people with hope.
Amen.

DAY 3

My Day Begins

Joan said, "The voice was the voice of St. Catherine and of St. Margaret. And their heads were crowned in a rich and precious fashion with beautiful crowns. And to tell this, I have God's permission. If you doubt it, send to Poitiers where I was examined before."

Asked how she knew one from the other, Joan answered, "I know them by the greeting they give me. A good seven years have passed since they undertook to guide me. I know the saints because they tell their names."

Asked which of the apparitions came to her first, she answered, "St. Michael came first."

Asked whether it was a long time ago that she first heard the voice of St. Michael, she answered, "I do not speak of St. Michael's voice, but of his presence that gave me great comfort."

All Through the Day

I am part of the cloud of witnesses, one with the saints who have gone before me.

My Day Is Ending

Lord, you call me to holiness,
but you do not call me alone.
Heaven is filled with saints of every age and era,
from every place and people,
of every virtue and vocation, personality and gift.
When I look at them, sometimes I feel small.
The pedestal upon which I have placed them is so high
I can't imagine how their lives were anything like mine.
Did they ever look to the saints who came before them
and feel small too?
Were they always so strong?
So sure?
So quick to do your will?
And if not, what mysterious force set their souls on
fire?
It had to be love.
Love empowered them to do the impossible.
Love led them to sacrifice.
Love held them rapt in prayer.
Love moved them close to the poor.
Love made some speak and drew others into silence.
Lord, give me guides who show me how to love.
Make me a lover, and I will be a saint.
Amen.

DAY 4

My Day Begins

The voice taught me to be good and to go to church often. And it told me that I must come to France. This voice told me once or twice a week that I should leave and come to France, and my father knew nothing of my leaving. The voice told me to come, and I could no longer stay where I was. And the voice told me again that I must raise the siege of the city of Orléans.

The voice told me, Joan, that I must go to Robert de Baudricourt in the town of Vaucouleurs where he was captain, and that he would provide me an escort. I answered that I was a poor maiden, knowing nothing of riding or fighting. I went to my uncle and told him that I wanted to stay with him for some time, and I stayed there about eight days. I told my uncle that I must go to the town of Vaucouleurs, and so he took me there.

All Through the Day

Lord, help me to discover your plan for my life.

My Day Is Ending

I learned to say, "Thy will be done."
But in the secret places of my heart, I whisper, "My will, not thine, Lord. Mine."
I hold my plans and dreams tightly.
I plot and scheme for what I want without considering the purpose you have for me,
the mission you wish to give me,
the life you have prepared for me.
Sometimes, Lord, I catch myself believing that your plans are for other people,
that you could never use someone like me.
Lord, help me to serve you the way you want to be served:
to leave my own ambitions behind,
to set my fears aside,
to move when you tell me,
to go where you send me,
to do whatever you ask.
Direct my steps and teach me to trust that you will put me to good use,
despite my lack of skill,
my inexperience,
my doubts.

Give me the courage to let you set my course,
to be bold when I am not,
to achieve what I cannot even imagine.
Amen.

DAY 5

My Day Begins

Asked if she had not spoken to her priest or any other churchman of the visions which she claimed to have, Joan answered, "No, except to Robert de Baudricourt and to my king. The voices did not compel me to conceal them, but I was afraid of revealing them, afraid that the Burgundians might hinder my journey. In particular, I feared that my father would stop it."

Asked if she believed it was right to leave her father and mother without permission, when she should honor her father and mother, Joan answered, "In all other things I was obedient to them, except in this journey. But afterwards, I wrote to them, and they forgave me."

Asked whether she thought she had committed a sin when she left her father and mother, she answered, "Since God commanded, it was right to do so. Since God commanded, if I had had a hundred parents, or had been the king's daughter, I would have gone nevertheless."

All Through the Day

Help me to do whatever God commands.

My Day Is Ending

Lord,
Sometimes, I don't say the things that should be said,
or hesitate to ask for forgiveness because I fear rejection.
Instruct me in your ways, Lord.
Sustain me when I do not understand exactly what you
are asking of me.
Give me a heart that is quick to obey.
Correct me when my judgment is in error.
Keep me from sin.
Lord, teach me to know your commands.
Inspire me with the urgency of your purpose.
Empower me to overcome any obstacles that arise.
Reassure me when I am uncertain.
Reveal the nature of true obedience to me.
Prepare me to accept any sacrifices I must make.
Show me how to keep your will at the center of my life.
Reign as king over all my decisions and deeds.
And keep me always in your service.
Amen.

DAY 6

My Day Begins

TESTIMONY OF JEAN DE METZ, JOAN'S CLOSEST OFFICER

When Joan was at Vaucouleurs, I saw her in a red dress, poor and worn. I said to her, "What are you doing here, my friend? Is it fate that the king must be driven from the kingdom and are we all to be English?"

"I have come here," she answered, "to this royal town to speak to Robert de Baudricourt so that he will conduct me or have me conducted to the king. But Robert cares neither about me nor my words. Nevertheless, before the middle of Lent, I must be with the king—even if I have to wear down my legs to the knees! No one in the world—not kings, nor dukes, nor the daughter of the king of Scotland, nor anyone else—can recover the kingdom of France. There will be no aid except from me. Nevertheless, I would rather spin at home with my poor mother—for this is not my proper place. It is, however, necessary that I should go and do this, because my Lord wills that

I should do it." And when I asked her who this Lord was, she told me it was God.

All Through the Day

Lord, when I encounter obstacles, strengthen me to persevere.

My Day Is Ending

Faithful and loving God, give me perseverance in whatever you ask of me.
Help me to know which things I should accept and which I should work to change.
Keep me centered on your will, especially when things do not go smoothly.
Guard me in humility when others refuse to listen,
when they do not understand your word to me
or are skeptical of the mission you have entrusted to me.
Do not let my fervor be extinguished by doubt.
Do not allow me to be distracted by a desire for approval,
but help me to find my identity and affirmation in you.

Lord,
Show me how to be both gentle and tenacious.
Both persistent and patient.
Give me unwavering trust in your word
and the courage that comes from firm convictions.
Keep me docile to your Holy Spirit.
Teach me to rely on your strength when I am weak,
your grace when I am overwhelmed,
and your peace when I am frustrated or confused.
Sustain me in faith, and keep me faithful in your
service.
Amen.

DAY 7

My Day Begins

TESTIMONY OF CATHERINE LEROYER

I knew Joan well; she was an excellent girl, simple, gentle, respectful, well-conducted, and loved to go to Church. She lived with us for about three weeks. When Robert de Baudricourt refused to escort her, she told me that she would go nevertheless and seek the dauphin. She said, "Do you not know the prophecy which says that France, lost by a woman, shall be saved by a maiden from the Marches of Lorraine?" I did indeed remember the prophecy and was astonished.

TESTIMONY OF HENRI LEROYER

At Vaucouleurs, Joan received the gift of men's clothing and complete equipment; then, mounted on a horse, she was conducted to the place where the dauphin was. When she spoke of leaving, she was asked how she thought she could make such a journey and escape the enemy. "I do not fear them," she answered, "I have a sure road. If the enemy are on my road, I have God with me, who knows how to prepare the way to the dauphin. I was born to do this!"

All Through the Day

When you are with me, Lord, I have nothing to fear.

My Day Is Ending

Sometimes, Lord, I am afraid.
I cannot see the path ahead.
I do not know where the way will lead me.
I am not certain of my purpose.
And yet, your voice calls me forward,
to take courage and trust in you completely.

Sometimes, in those moments, I struggle.
My legs are too heavy, and my mind too slow.
My fears swirl within me.
They hold me captive where I am.
They taunt me and say, "You are alone. You are too small."

Yet you, O God, are with me.
And no path is too difficult for you.
You are the one who sets my course.
It is you who guards and guides me.

Open the road before me and teach my heart to set fear aside.
Help me to follow you in faith,
even when darkness falls,
even when the enemy surrounds me on every side.
Reveal your plan for my life, Lord.
Confirm my purpose.
And give me all the grace I need to accomplish your holy will.
Amen.

DAY 8

My Day Begins

TESTIMONY OF SEGUIN SEGUIN, THE DOMINICAN FRIAR WHO EXAMINED JOAN AT POITIERS

I told the Maid, "God wills that you should not be believed unless some sign appears to prove that you ought to be believed; and we shall not advise the king to trust in you and to risk an army on your simple statement."

"In God's name!" Joan replied. "I have not come to Poitiers to show signs: but send me to Orléans, where I shall show you the signs by which I am sent." And she added: "Send me enough men as may seem good, and I will go to Orléans."

And then she foretold to us—to me and to all the others who were with me—these four things which should happen, and which did afterwards come to pass: first, that the English would be destroyed, the siege of Orléans raised, and the town delivered from the English; secondly, that the king would be crowned at Rheims; thirdly, that Paris would be restored to his dominion; and fourthly, that the Duke of Orléans should be brought back from England. And I have seen these four things accomplished.

All Through the Day

God keeps his promises.

My Day Is Ending

Lord, sometimes I am dragged down by uncertainty
and doubt.
Even when I have seen you at work, there are times I
don't truly believe that you will keep your word to me.
Show me your faithfulness.
Lord, give me a heart ready to believe.
Help me to put my suspicions to rest.
Guide me in discerning who and what can be trusted.
Keep my mind open to all your works, even those that
are prophetic or mystical.
Send me signs of your presence when I need them, but
do not allow me to be deceived.
Do not send me ill-equipped or unprepared.
Train me how to hear and know your voice.
Never let me put my words into your mouth.
Help me to listen with the intent to obey.
Form me in faith that is prudent and firm.
Let me undertake only what you ask of me.

Guard me from pride, from the desire to be important,
from a hunger for attention or acclaim.
Use my life as an instrument of your will.
Make me a messenger of your love.
Amen.

DAY 9

My Day Begins

Joan said, "When I was at Tours or Chinon, I sent for a sword, which was in the church of Sainte-Catherine-de-Fierbois, behind the altar; and immediately it was found there all rusted over." Asked how she knew the sword was there, Joan answered, "The sword was in the ground, rusted over, and upon it were five crosses. I knew it was there through my voices, and I had never seen the man who fetched it. I wrote to the clergy of the place asking if it was their pleasure that I should have the sword, and they sent it to me. It was not buried deep behind the altar, but I believe I wrote saying it was behind. As soon as the sword was found, the priests rubbed it and the rust fell off at once without effort."

Asked what blessing she said or asked over the sword, Joan answered, "I never blessed it myself or had it blessed. I would not have known how. I loved the sword since it had been found in the church of St. Catherine, whom I love."

All Through the Day

God will give me everything I need to do what he asks of me.

My Day Is Ending

Lord, sometimes I feel unworthy of your plans for me.
I worry about whether I am up to the task.
I am anxious about having what I need to answer your call.
Calm my heart, O God, and help me to trust completely in your providence.
Supply everything necessary for me to do your will.
Give me knowledge, wisdom, and skill.
Provide whatever resources and tools are needed.
Show me how to make good use of all you have given me.
Keep me from wasting time.
Guard me from coveting what others possess.
Do not allow me to chase after things I do not need.
Draw me always to your altar.
Reveal to me what is hidden.
Remind me to carry your blessings with me.
Teach me to treasure what I have, to count everything as coming from your hand.
Amen.

DAY 10

My Day Begins

TESTIMONY OF SIMON CHARLES, PRESIDENT OF THE CHAMBER OF ACCOUNTS

When Joan came to Chinon, some of the King's Council said that the king ought not to put faith in this Joan; others said that, because she declared she was sent from God and commanded to speak to the king, the king ought at least to hear her.

When the king knew that she was coming, he withdrew to one side, stepping back from the others. But Joan clearly recognized him and bowed to him; she had a long meeting with him. After he had heard her, the king appeared joyful. Then the king, not wishing to do anything without the advice of the ecclesiastics, sent Joan to the town of Poitiers so that she might be examined by the clerks of the university. After the king learned that she had been investigated and nothing had been found in her except good, he had her armed and gave men to her; she also received control over military affairs.

All Through the Day

Let there be no conflict between my actions and my words.

My Day Is Ending

Make me a person of integrity, Lord.
May my words be confirmed by my deeds:
by the choices I make, the example I set, and the way I treat others.
Purify my faith.
Make my witness clear.
Train me in virtue and the works of your mercy.

Lord, let no one find anything but good in me.
Teach me how to answer every question honestly,
to submit myself humbly to any examination.
Guard me from hypocrisy, from presenting a false or flattering image of myself.
Perfect your image in my soul.
Guide me according to your purpose and plan.
Help me to see things the way you see them.

Keep me focused, Lord, on accomplishing your will.
Bring me to those who long to see your face,

to those who seek the fullness of peace.
And reveal yourself to them through me.
Amen.

DAY 11

My Day Begins

TESTIMONY OF JEAN II, DUKE OF ALENÇON

Many times, and in my presence, Joan told the king she would last one year and no more and that he should consider how to best use this year. She said, "I have four duties to accomplish: to beat the English; to have the king crowned and consecrated at Rheims; to deliver the Duke of Orléans from the hands of the English; and to raise the siege of Orléans.

LETTER OF JOAN OF ARC TO THE KING OF ENGLAND

+ Jesus Mary +
King of England, make satisfaction to the King of Heaven. The Maid is very ready to make peace, if you are willing to grant her satisfaction by means of rendering justice to France and paying for what you have held. Go back to your own country, by God. I have been sent to drive you out of all France. If your men wish to obey, I will show them mercy. If you do not wish to believe the news from God and the Maid, then wherever we find you, we will

strike and raise a war cry greater than any there has been in France for a thousand years.

All Through the Day

Make good use of the time I have.

My Day Is Ending

Loving and faithful God, you know me better than I know myself.
You hold the plan and purpose of my life.
Reveal the mission you have for me and
give me the grace to place my life into your hands.
Show me how to carry out all that you have placed on my shoulders.
Help me to fight for justice boldly,
to show mercy tenderly.
Give me a heart that is always ready to forge peace.

Lord, teach me to use well the time you have given me.
Guide me in setting priorities.
Keep me faithful to your call.
Make me confident in your plan.

Protect me.
Let it always be enough for me to know that you have sent me:
into my family to love you,
into my country to serve you,
into the world to make you known.
Amen.

DAY 12

My Day Begins

Asked whether, when she went to Orléans, she had standard or banner, Joan answered, "I had a banner with a field sown with lilies; the world was depicted on it, and two angels, one on each side. It was fine white linen. On it, I think, were written the names Jesus and Mary; and it was fringed with silk."

Asked which she cared for most, her banner or her sword, Joan answered: "I love my banner better, forty times better than my sword." Asked who made her get this painting done upon her banner, she answered: "I have told you often enough that I have done nothing but by the command of God. It was I myself who bore this banner when I attacked the enemy to keep from killing anyone, and I never have killed anyone."

All Through the Day

Lord, help me to do everything in your name and for your glory.

My Day Is Ending

King of Heaven, reign over me.
Let my life extend your kingdom.
I place myself under your banner.
I dedicate all my words and actions to your glory, and not my own.
Teach me how to act in your name—Jesus—and in the name of your holy mother, Mary.
Never let me harm anyone, not even an adversary.
Give me reverence for all who bear your image.
Help me to live a life of faithful service to you.
Keep me from serving my own preferences and interests.
Guard my soul from pride and vainglory.
Prevent me from taking credit.
Protect me from the desire to influence others.
Preserve me from sin.
Paint your image on the standard of my heart.
Let me do only what you command.
For you are God.
All creation praises you.
All times belong to you.
All things serve your holy will.
All the saints adore you.

All the angels bow before your throne.

Amen.

DAY 13

My Day Begins

TESTIMONY OF SQUIRE SIMON BEAUCROIX

In war time, Joan would not permit any of those in her company to steal anything; nor would she ever eat of food which she knew to be stolen. Once, a Scotsman told her that he had eaten meat from a stolen calf: she was very angry and wanted to strike the Scot for so doing.

Joan would never permit women of ill repute to follow the army; none of them dared to come into her presence; but, if any of them did appear, she made them depart unless the soldiers were willing to marry them.

She was good not only to the French but also to the enemy. All this I know with certainty, for I was with Joan for a long time, and many times I assisted in arming her.

She lamented much and was displeased when good women came wishing to greet her. She was angry about it because it seemed to her like adoration.

TESTIMONY OF JEAN BARBIN, DOCTOR OF LAW, KING'S ADVOCATE

All the soldiers held Joan as sacred. So well did she bear herself in warfare, in words, and in deeds as a follower of God that no evil could be said of her.

All Through the Day

Does my goodness inspire others to be virtuous?

My Day Is Ending

Lord, you are holy.
And though we are sinners, separated from you,
you call us to yourself.
Guide me along the path to holiness.
Give me patience with myself and others.
Do not allow a spirit of judgment or condemnation to grow within me.
Keep me from all self-righteousness.
Fill me with your goodness and truth.
Help me to cultivate virtue in myself
and inspire others to live according to your law.
Let me lead more by example than by words.
Give me gentleness when I guide another.

Make me aware of my own shortfalls and sins.
Do not allow me to be deceived.
Keep me from excusing or minimizing sin.
Prevent me from accommodating evil or making any provision for wrongdoing.
Strengthen me to drive all evil away.
Help me to hold on to you alone.
Grant me a sincere love for sinners.
Make me willing to do what I can to rescue them from self-destruction,
to open the gates of heaven wide,
and to reach for heaven from the edge of hell.
Amen.

DAY 14

My Day Begins

TESTIMONY OF JEAN II, DUKE OF ALENÇON

When it was decided to attack, the heralds-at-arms began to sound, "To the Assault!" "Forward, gentle duke, to the assault!" Joan cried to me. And when I told her it was premature to attack so quickly, she said: "Have no fear. The right time is when it pleases God. We must work when it is his will. Act, and God will act!" Later, she said to me, "Ah! Gentle duke, are you afraid? Don't you know that I promised your wife to bring you back, safe and sound?"

During the assault on Jargeau, Joan said to me: "Go back from this place, or that engine"—pointing out a piece of artillery in the city—"will kill you." I retired, and shortly after that engine did indeed kill a man named de Lude in the same place she had told me to leave. Because of this, I had great fear, and I wondered at Joan's words and how they came true.

All Through the Day

I will surrender my doubts to God and act trusting in him.

My Day Is Ending

Lord, sometimes I am paralyzed by fear or uncertainty.
I wait for the right time, and it never seems to come.
In my doubts, I hesitate.
Sometimes, I fail to act at all.
Calm my anxiety, Lord.
Teach me how to set misgivings aside.
Help me to trust you—and your Spirit within me—
more deeply.
Give me courage in place of reluctance.
Overcome my indecision with faith.
Strengthen my wavering resolve.
Make me swift to obey your will.
When my next step is clear, help me to take it,
with hope,
with confidence,
despite any apprehension or disbelief.
Give me the grace to follow you, and not to lead.

Keep me from forcing your hand
or substituting my plans for yours.
Show me that when I act, I do not act alone,
that you are always with me,
that you are there to guide me,
that you will uphold and strengthen me,
that you, too, will act in my life.
Help me to see when the hour is ripe.
Free me from the fears that tell me to wait.

Prepare me to act wholly according to your will,
not only in what I do but also when.
Amen.

DAY 15

My Day Begins

TESTIMONY OF MILITARY CAPTAIN JEAN, COUNT OF DUNOIS

The twenty-seventh of May, very early in the morning, we began the attack on the Boulevard of the bridge. There, Joan was wounded by an arrow which penetrated half a foot between her neck and shoulder. Nonetheless, she continued to fight and took no remedy for her wound. The attack lasted from the morning until eight o'clock in the evening without hope of success. For this reason, I was anxious that the army should retire into the town.

Joan then came to me, asking that I wait a little longer. Thereupon she mounted her horse, rode to a vineyard all alone by herself, and remained in prayer about half an hour. Then, returning and seizing her banner with both hands, she placed herself on the edge of the trench. At sight of her, the English trembled and were seized with sudden fear. Our people, on the contrary, took courage and began to mount and assail the Boulevard, not meeting any resistance. The Boulevard was taken and the English put to flight. All of them were killed, including a principal

English captain who had spoken of the Maid with the greatest contempt and insult.

All Through the Day

I can be victorious despite my own weaknesses and wounds.

My Day Is Ending

Loving and faithful God,
When I am wounded, or suffer pain,
heal me and restore what I have lost.
Soothe and comfort me in my brokenness.
Breathe new life into my soul.
Help me to forgive, and to trust again.

Help me to recognize the wounds of others,
to strengthen and support them in the challenges they face,
to share their burdens,
to fight beside them,
to be an instrument of your healing love.

Grant me the courage to rejoin the fight, to take up your banner again.
May I never withdraw from the battles to which you have called me.
May I never retreat or give up because I am weak or afraid.
For you, Lord, are mighty.
No one snatches victory from your hand.

Draw me into your presence.
Guide me in prayer.
Help me to take my place again on the field,
when the time is right and only under your command.
Amen.

DAY 16

My Day Begins

TESTIMONY OF JOAN'S CONFESSOR, JEAN PASQUEREL

After dinner, the other priests went with me to seek Joan at her residence. When we arrived, we heard her calling out, "Where are the men who should arm me? The blood of our people is falling to the ground!" And as soon as she was armed, she left the town and made for where the attack was taking place. On the road, Joan met many wounded soldiers; the sight of them greatly distressed her. She went to the assault and did so well that by force and violence the fort was at last taken, and all the English who were there were taken prisoners. I remember that this took place on the eve of the Ascension of Our Savior.

When the fort was taken, the English died there in great numbers. Joan was much afflicted when she heard they had died without confession and pitied them. She made her own confession on the spot and ordered me to invite the whole army to do likewise and give thanks to God for the victory just gained. "Otherwise," she said, "I will no longer help them, or even remain with them."

All Through the Day

I will not withhold compassion, even from my enemies.

My Day Is Ending

Lord, you are merciful.
You teach me to show compassion,
even toward those who are my adversaries.
Give me tears for all who are far from you.
Even in victory, may I never lose sight of what others are suffering.
Fill my heart with pity for those who have not been given the grace to set things right,
to repent of their sins,
to make reparation,
to forgive or ask for forgiveness.
Keep me humble, even in battle.
Teach me to respect the humanity of my enemies,
to tread lightly where others have lost,
to care for the wounded,
to honor the dead and pray for them.
Keep me from taking your grace for granted.
Guide me, Lord, to seek you while I can.

Do not allow me to forego a kindness,
delay confessing my sins,
or hold back forgiveness from anyone who asks.
Show me how to meet you here and now,
where I am,
wherever you have placed me.
Amen.

DAY 17

My Day Begins

TESTIMONY OF MILITARY CAPTAIN JEAN, COUNT OF DUNOIS

The army escorting the convoy did not appear to me or to the other captains sufficient to resist the English. To reach Orléans, it was necessary to sail against the stream, and the wind was altogether contrary.

Then Joan said to me, "Is it you who said I should come on this side of the river, and not go directly to where the English are?"

"Yes, and those wiser than I are of the same opinion, for our greater success and safety."

"In God's name," Joan said, "the counsel of my Lord is safer and wiser than yours. You thought to deceive me, but it is you who are deceived, for I bring you better aid than has ever come to any general or town whatsoever—the help of the King of Heaven. This does not come from me but from God himself, who, at the prayers of St. Louis and St. Charlemagne, has had compassion on the town of Orléans and will not suffer the enemy to hold at both the duke and his town!"

At that moment, the wind, which had prevented the boats going up the river and reaching Orléans, turned all at once and became favorable.

All Through the Day

God is the source of my wisdom.

My Day Is Ending

Lord, bless those who love me enough to share their wisdom with me,
to give me the benefit of their experience,
to assist me with their advice.
But help me to find wisdom in you.
When the winds are against me, teach me to trust.
You are in control, and all the universe is subject to you.
You will do all you have said.

Lord, give me the wisdom I need to accomplish my mission.
Let me never doubt the word you have given me.
Make me a witness to your fidelity.

Teach me to act with complete abandonment to your perfect will,
with faith in your power,
with total trust in your promise.
Help me to believe in your goodness and the plan you have marked out for me.
Show me how to rely on your help,
so that I may experience the full splendor of your glory.
Amen.

DAY 18

My Day Begins

TESTIMONY OF KNIGHT AND MILITARY CAPTAIN THIBAULD D'ARMAGNAC

Joan had predicted that few or none of the French would be killed or suffer loss. This happened, for of all our men only one gentleman of my company perished. Apart from affairs of war, she was simple and innocent. But in the conduct and disposition of troops and in actual warfare, in the ordering of battle and in animating the soldiers, she behaved as the most skilled captain in the world who had been trained in the art of war all his life.

TESTIMONY OF JEAN II, DUKE OF ALENÇON

In all she did except in affairs of war, Joan was a very simple young girl; but for warlike things—bearing the lance, assembling an army, ordering military operations, and directing artillery—she was most skillful. Everyone wondered how she could act with as much wisdom and foresight as a captain who had fought for twenty or thirty years. Above all, she was wonderful in making use of artillery.

All Through the Day

God will train and equip me to do his will.

My Day Is Ending

Lord,
Nothing is an obstacle to you.
You know everything.
Sometimes, I shudder at what is new or unfamiliar.
Help me to see that if it is your will, I need not fear.
You will provide all I need to do what you ask of me.

I can walk in confidence.
You are with me and will not allow me to stumble.
You will not set me up to fail.
You alone are enough.

Show me the gifts you have hidden within me,
gifts yet undiscovered and unopened.
You are the God of the impossible.
There is nothing beyond your reach.
You lead me to joy and victory on unexpected paths.
Amen.

DAY 19

My Day Begins

TESTIMONY OF JOAN'S HOSTESS, MARGUERITE LA TOUROULDE

The town of Orléans was besieged, and there was no help. In this calamity, Joan came, and I firmly believe that she came from God and was sent for the relief of the king and his faithful subjects, who then were without hope except in God.

She remained with me for three weeks—sleeping, drinking, and eating. Nearly every night I slept with her, and I never perceived any evil in her. Joan carried herself as a worthy and Catholic woman, often confessing herself, willingly hearing Mass, and many times asking me to accompany her to matins, which at her request I often did.

I remember that many women came to my house while Joan was there and brought rosaries and other religious objects that she might touch them. But Joan laughed, saying: "Touch them yourselves. Your touch will do them as much good as mine."

Joan was very liberal in almsgiving, and willingly helped the poor and indigent, saying that she had been sent for their consolation.

All Through the Day

Lord, make me your true disciple.

My Day Is Ending

Loving and faithful God, this world is full of misery.
Families are strained.
Children are anxious.
The elderly are lonely.
Many are imprisoned by addiction.
Those who are poor struggle against homelessness and hunger.
Violence and war are everywhere.
And hope can hardly be found.

My faith is nothing special.
I can't begin to touch the depth of the darkness.
But Lord, when I ask you to intervene,
you whisper to my heart.
You tell me that you will send me,
and if I go, that I will find that you are already there.

Increase your charity in me, Lord.
Enough that I will stop waiting for someone else.
Enough that I will go myself,
with nothing less than the One I take with me.
Amen.

DAY 20

My Day Begins

TESTIMONY OF MILITARY CAPTAIN JEAN, COUNT OF DUNOIS

After the deliverance of Orléans, the king was in his private room and Joan and I went to seek him. As soon as she had entered, she knelt before the king, and, embracing his knees, said: "Noble dauphin! Hold these many and long councils no more but come quickly to Rheims to take the crown for which you are worthy!"

"Will you not say, here in presence of the king," added the bishop, "what kind of counsel speaks this to you?"

Then Joan blushed as she said, "When I am vexed that faith is not readily placed in what I wish to say in God's name, I retire alone and pray to God. I complain to him that those whom I address do not believe me more readily. When my prayer ends, I hear a voice which says to me: 'Daughter of God! Go on! Go on! I will be your help: go on!' When I hear this, I have great joy and wish I could always hear the voice this way." And in repeating the words of her voice to us, Joan was—strange to say!—in a marvelous rapture, raising her eyes to heaven.

All Through the Day

I am a child of God.

My Day Is Ending

Lord, guide me when things are not going well.
Draw me away to seek your counsel.
Quiet my heart to pray.
Help me to hear your voice amid trouble and misfortune.
Sustain me through difficulty.
Keep me firm in faith.
Reassure me of your presence and the task you have placed in my hands.

And when you will it,
awaken my heart.
Move me forward.
Send me.

Give me your help, Lord.
And I will be filled with joy.
Because I am yours,
nothing can stop me from accomplishing your will.
Because I am your child, I cannot fail.
Amen.

DAY 21

My Day Begins

TESTIMONY OF MILITARY CAPTAIN JEAN, COUNT OF DUNOIS

When the king came, the people ran around him, crying "Noel!" The Maid was then riding between the archbishop of Rheims and myself. "This is a good people," she said to us. "I have seen none elsewhere who rejoiced as much at the coming of so noble a king. How happy should I be if, when my days are done, I might be buried here!"

"Joan," the archbishop said to her, "in what place do you hope to die?"

"Where it shall please God," she answered. "For I am not certain of either the time or the place, any more than you are yourself. If only it would please God, my Creator, that I might retire now, abandon arms and return to serve my father and mother and tend their sheep with my sister and my brothers, who would be so happy to see me again!"

All Through the Day

Help me to surrender my whole life to your will.

My Day Is Ending

Loving and faithful God,
I do not often consider how or when my life will end.
There are too many unknowns.
Help me, Lord, so that at the end of my life,
there will not be
too many things I wish I had done,
too many things I wish I could change.

Lord,
Help me to live in the fullness of every moment.
Teach me how to receive the gift of each day.
Show me how to give myself entirely to your purpose.
Help me to love all I encounter, especially those who are closest to me.
Keep me faithful to the word you have spoken to me.

Lord, you will measure the mission of my life.
It is you who will tell me when to lay down my arms.
Give me the grace to surrender myself entirely to your will:

body, mind, soul, and spirit.
And at the end of my life, let nothing remain,
nothing but the final breath that places me in your hands forever.
Amen.

DAY 22

My Day Begins

TESTIMONY OF KNIGHT RAIMOND DE MACY

Joan was taken to Rouen and placed in a prison facing the fields. The Count of Ligny said to her: "Joan, I have come to ransom you if you will promise never again to bear arms against us."

Joan answered, "In God's name, you mock me, for I know that you have neither the will nor the power. I know the English will send me to death, thinking that then they will gain the kingdom of France. But if they were a hundred thousand more numerous, they would still never have the kingdom."

TESTIMONY OF COURT NOTARY GUILLAUME MANCHON

Before the bishop of Beauvais took the case, Joan was put in irons. She was treated cruelly and, toward the end of the trial, threatened with torture. Joan wore men's clothing and dared not remove them because she feared the guards might assault her.

All Through the Day

Preserve me, Lord, and keep me faithful and pure.

My Day Is Ending

Lord, you know how cruel people can be.
When you were arrested, you were imprisoned and mocked.
You suffered injustice and torture at the hands of your enemies.
Even your closest friends abandoned you.

Remind me to turn to you when I am mistreated.
Sustain me through every difficulty.
Strengthen me when I feel threatened.
Protect the purity of my body and soul.
Help me to pray for those who persecute me.
Fill me with hope even when things are unfair.

Give me the courage to stand up for others.
Do not allow me to remain silent or tolerate abuse in any form.
Show me how to guard the dignity of every person.
Inspire me to work for justice.

Keep me free from the desire for revenge.
Amen.

DAY 23

My Day Begins

TESTIMONY OF COURT NOTARY GUILLAUME MANCHON

At the beginning of the trial, the judges, speaking in Latin several times, wished to compel me to rewrite the Maid's answers and explanations by changing the sense of her words or in other ways that did not represent what I had heard. By command of the bishop, two men were placed at a window near where the judges sat, with a curtain across the window, so that they could not be seen. These two men wrote and reported the charges against Joan, and they kept silent regarding her defense. Afterward, while comparing notes of what had been written, the two others had reported differently from me and had included none of the testimony in her favor. In recording the process, I was often opposed by the bishop of Beauvais and the masters, who wanted to compel me to write according to their fancy and against what I had myself heard.

TESTIMONY OF DOMINICAN FRIAR ISAMBART DE LA PIERRE

Judging from the case and all that was done in connection with it, it is my belief and judgment that the English acted against Joan out of hatred and malice and that they had no other purpose than her death.

All Through the Day

God, keep me from despair.

My Day Is Ending

Lord, sometimes it seems that corruption is everywhere.
Selfishness obscures the common good.
The drive for wealth and power perverts our institutions.
Justice is lost, and deception rules the day.

How can you allow those who are evil to prosper?
Why do you let them devour those who love you?
I am tempted to lose hope.

Yet I know that your justice will ultimately triumph.
Teach me to love the world the way you do,
to see beyond the corruption,
to believe that what was once good can be good again.
Help me to live in peace amid the fallenness,
in truth regardless of the fraud,
in joy despite the decay.
And free me from all that corrodes and corrupts.
Amen.

DAY 24

My Day Begins

Asked if she wished to submit all her acts or sayings, either good or evil, to the decision of Our Mother the Church, Joan answered, "I love the Church and would support it with all my might for the Christian faith. I am not a person to be forbidden to go to church or hear Mass." As for the good works she did and her coming, Joan said, "I commit myself to the King of Heaven who sent me to Charles, son of Charles, King of France, who should be king of France. And you will see that the people of France will soon win a great undertaking which God will send and which will shake almost the whole kingdom of France."

Asked whether she would submit to the decision of the Church, she answered, "I commit myself to Our Lord who sent me, Our Lady, and all the blessed saints of paradise. It seems to me that Our Lord and the Church are all one. Why do you make difficulties when it is all one?"

All Through the Day

Give me a sincere love for the Church.

My Day Is Ending

Lord, you are easy to love.
You created me and continually sustain me.
You save and sanctify me.
You count me among your children and fill me with your grace.
There is no end to your goodness and mercy.
You are a loving and faithful Father.

You have called the Church your body and bride.
You have given her to us as a nurturing mother.
But she doesn't always reflect your goodness.
There are times when the Church is unkind.
Times when she fails to defend what is right.
Times when she is no better than the world.
That's why it isn't always easy to love her.
That's why it isn't always easy to obey her.

Make my love for the Church resilient and deep.
May I never treat your people as anything less than your beloved.
Empower me to remain charitable, even in times of frustration or disappointment.
Keep me from abandoning the community of your faithful.

Let all I say and do foster unity among all Christians.
Help me to hold on to the truth that you and your
Church are one and the same.
Amen.

DAY 25

My Day Begins

Asked if she believes it displeasing to God to speak the truth, Joan answered, "My voices told me to say certain things to the king and not to you."

Asked why this voice no longer speaks with the king as it did when Joan was in his presence, she said, "I do not know whether it is the will of God. Except for the will of God, I could do nothing."

Asked whether the voice of which she asked counsel had sight and eyes, Joan answered, "There is a saying among little children: Men are sometimes hanged for telling the truth."

Asked if she knows she is in God's grace, Joan answered, "If I am not, may God put me there; and if I am, may God so keep me. I should be the saddest creature in the world if I knew I were not in his grace. But if I were in a state of sin, I do not think the voice would come to me. And I wish that everyone could hear the voice as well as I do."

All Through the Day

Except for God's grace, I could do nothing.

My Day Is Ending

Loving and faithful God,
I know that I could do nothing without you.
But I have also seen that with you, all things are possible.
You are a God who works wonders.
Lord, lead me to the font of your grace and keep me there.
Preserve me from sin.
Never let me be far from you.
And when I wander, bring me back.
Lord, shower me with your grace.
Give me everything I need to fulfill your plan for my life,
to accomplish your will,
to complete the mission you have placed into my hands.
Guide me always.
Remain with me.
Help me to please you in all things.
Let me bring glory to your holy name
and make you known to all I meet.
Amen.

DAY 26

My Day Begins

Joan said, "I asked the voice to counsel me in my replies and told the voice to seek the counsel of Our Lord. And the voice told me to answer boldly and God would comfort me."

Asked if the voice had not spoken certain words to her before she questioned it, she replied, "The voice spoke certain words, but I did not understand them all. However, when I awakened from sleep, the voice told me to answer boldly."

TESTIMONY OF JEAN MASSIEU, WHO USHERED JOAN TO HER EXECUTION

I remember that incomplete questions were often put to Joan, and many and difficult interrogations were made together. Then, before she could answer one, another would ask a question, so that she was displeased, saying, "Speak one after the other." I was amazed that she could so answer the subtle and entrapping questions put to her. No man of letters could have replied better.

All Through the Day

I will answer boldly and trust that God will help me.

My Day Is Ending

Lord, I don't have all the answers.
There are limits to what I know, even limits to what I can know.
Give me your counsel and your help.
Help me to hear your voice above the rest.
Teach me how to answer the questions that are prompted by my faith,
the people who are challenged by my life,
and any who make themselves my adversaries.

Give me the courage to speak boldly,
to give a clear and honest account.
Not to deceive.
Not to exaggerate.
Not to exercise influence.
May all my words glow with the light of your truth.

Help me to understand your word to me.
Guard me from confusion or misconception.

Guide me in discerning what to disclose and what to keep to myself.
Give me wisdom.
Surround me with your peace.
Amen.

DAY 27

My Day Begins

Joan said, "You say that you are my judge; I do not know if you are, but take good heed not to judge me wrongly, because you would put yourself in great peril. And I warn you so that if God punishes you for it, I shall have done my duty in telling you."

Asked what the peril or danger was, Joan answered, "St. Catherine told me I would have aid. I do not know whether this will be my deliverance from prison or if, while I am being tried, some tumult might come through which I can be delivered. I think it will be one or the other. Beyond this, the voices have told me I will be delivered by a great victory. Then they said, 'Take it all peacefully: have no care for your martyrdom; in the end you will come to the kingdom of paradise.' The voices told me simply and absolutely, that is, without faltering. My martyrdom is the pain and adversity I suffer in prison. I do not know if I will suffer greater adversity, but I commit myself to God."

All Through the Day

Judgment belongs to God.

My Day Is Ending

Lord, you are the Eternal King, the one who will judge us all at the end of time.
Keep me from the danger of judging others wrongfully.
Do not allow me to believe that I know who should be exonerated and who condemned.
Prevent me from making myself anyone else's judge.

Deliver me, too, from the judgments others make of me.
Preserve me from distress.
Teach me to rely on your merciful help.
Keep me firm in faith.
Help me to trust that they have no power over me.
Give me the grace to remember that you rule the universe.
That you will uphold me because you love me.

Lord, be merciful to me.
Do not hold my sins or failings against me.
Help me to leave everything to you.
Give me the victory you have promised.
And lead me to heaven.
Amen.

DAY 28

My Day Begins

One of the theologians explained a passage from Matthew 18 to Joan in French, and she was finally told that if she would not submit to the Church and obey it, she would be abandoned as an infidel. Joan answered, "I am a good Christian and have been properly baptized, and so I will die a good Christian."

Asked why, since she requested the Church to administer the sacrament of the Eucharist to her, she would not submit to the Church Militant, as then she had been promised the sacrament, she answered, "As for submission, I will answer nothing different from my previous answers. I love God and am a good Christian, and I desire to aid and support the holy Church with all my strength."

Asked if she did not wish a fine and distinguished procession to be ordained to restore her to good standing if she were not there, she answered, "I much desire the Church and Catholics to pray for me."

All Through the Day

Lord, remind me to seek support and give it through prayer.

My Day Is Ending

Lord, teach me to pray.
When I cannot hear your voice,
when I don't know what to do,
when I am in distress,
when I feel alone,
when I am afraid,
when I'm overwhelmed,
Lord, teach me to pray.

Lord, teach me to pray.
When others cannot find you,
when they are tempted,
when they sin,
when they are needy,
when they are ill,
when they are dead,
Lord, teach me to pray.

Lord, help me to love you.
Help me to serve you.
Help me to live my Christian faith.
Help me to die in your grace.
And when I cannot pray,
Hear the prayers of others for me.
Amen.

DAY 29

My Day Begins

TESTIMONY OF JEAN MASSIEU, WHO USHERED JOAN TO HER EXECUTION

When Joan was handed over by the Church, I was still with her, and with great devotion she asked to have a cross. An Englishman who was there made a little cross of wood from the ends of a stick, which he gave her. She received and kissed it devoutly, making piteous lamentations and acknowledgments to God, our Redeemer, who had suffered on the cross for our redemption, of whose cross she had the sign and symbol. She put the cross on her breast, between her person and her clothing. She asked me humbly if I would get the church cross for her so that she might see it continually until death. She cried her last word before dying with a loud voice: "Jesus!"

TESTIMONY OF MARTIN LADVENU, DOMINICAN PRIEST WHO HEARD JOAN'S LAST CONFESSION

Joan was led by the executioner, without any sentence from the secular judges, to the place where the pile was prepared for her burning. The pile was on a scaffold, and the executioner lit it from below. When Joan perceived the fire, she told me, "Descend, and raise the cross of the Lord high so I can see it."

All Through the Day

Lord, help me to see your suffering in my own.

My Day Is Ending

Lord, I am grateful.
You have given me a purpose, a mission meant for me alone.
You have granted me countless blessings and victories in battles both decisive and small.
Your voice has guided me.
Your will has moved me.
Your love has filled me.
But I sometimes forget that following you will bring me to the Cross.
You show me that the crown I hope for can be found only there, in the sacrificial gift of self.

Lord, help me to embrace the Cross and teach me how to choose it.
Give me the courage to hold it close.
Enable me to offer my suffering in union with yours.
Raise the emblem of your victory over death high above me.
Help me to see it through the flames.
And may your name be the last word on my lips.
Amen.

DAY 30

My Day Begins

TESTIMONY OF JEAN RICQUIER, CATHEDRAL CHAPLAIN IN ROUEN

That morning, Joan asked Master Pierre, "Where shall I be this evening?" He replied, "Do you not have a good hope in God?" She answered, "I do, and with God's help, I will be in paradise."

TESTIMONY OF DOMINICAN FRIAR ISAMBART DE LA PIERRE

A certain English soldier hated Joan greatly. When he heard Joan calling on the name of Jesus in her last moments, he was astonished at the spectacle. That afternoon, the same Englishman confessed, in my presence, that he had gravely erred and repented of what he had done against Joan. He held her to be a good woman, for he had seen the spirit departing from her, a white dove flying away from France.

In the afternoon of the same day, the executioner came to the convent of the Dominicans, saying to them and to Br. Martin Ladvenu that he feared he was damned because he had burnt a saint.

TESTIMONY OF COURT NOTARY GUILLAUME MANCHON

Never did I weep more for anything that happened to me. And for a month afterwards I could not feel at peace. That is the reason I bought a little missal with part of the money I was paid for my services, so that I might have it to remind me to pray for the Maid. Regarding final repentance, I never saw greater signs of a Christian.

All Through the Day

Give me perseverance, Lord, to live my faith to the end.

My Day Is Ending

Loving and faithful God, you raise up great saints to inspire us,
to show us how to live,
to teach us virtue,
to uphold us in prayer,
to light the path before us,
to encourage us to allow you to transform our lives.

No one arrives in heaven without the aid of your grace.
No one enters your glory without seeking your mercy.
All of us are weak.
All of us have sinned.

Lord, give me the courage to strive for holiness.
Even when defeat seems inevitable,
even when I don't have the strength to go on,
even when my enemies surround me.
Help me to hear your voice always.
Give me a heart ready to do your will.
Make me holy.
And bring me to the eternal victory you have already secured for me.
Amen.

Nine-Year Novena Prayer

At the close of 2022, Catholic philosopher and essayist Thibaud Collin proposed a sustained campaign of prayer in France in anticipation of the six hundredth anniversary of Joan of Arc's death in 2031. The intention of this novena is the renewal of the Catholic faith in France, and each of the nine years highlights one of Joan's many virtues. To join this initiative, offer the prayer below daily. To learn more about it, visit jeanne2031.fr.

St. Joan of Arc,
Like you, we want to be faithful to the promises of our baptism;
guide us.
We want to discern the will of God to accomplish it;
enlighten us.
We desire to follow the standard of Christ to extend his reign over our lives, our homeland, and the Church;
go before us.
We implore you for the salvation of our country and our souls;
pray for us.
Amen.

One Final Word

This book was created to be nothing more than a gateway—a gateway to the spiritual wisdom of a specific teacher and a gateway opening for your own spiritual way.

You may decide that Joan of Arc is someone whose experience of God is one that you wish to follow more closely and deeply, in which case you should get a copy of one of the books quoted in this text and pray with it as you have prayed in this gateway journey.

You may decide that this experience has heightened your hunger for additional spiritual teachers, and you will encounter many on your own, very special, absolutely unique journey of the spirit. You will discover your path. We would not be searching, as St. Augustine reminds us, if we had not already been found.

Notes

The original transcripts of fifteenth-century legal records provide both the questions and the witness responses to those questions as reported speech. In the "My Day Begins" section of this book, the responses have been edited to present them in the form of direct, first-person testimony, which is how they were offered at the time. The notes below cite the official transcripts where these verbal exchanges may be found. While there are several translations of these documents from Latin and French, this book draws almost exclusively from sources in the public domain, with minimal adaptation for today's readers and the meditational format of this book.

DAY 1

Joan of Arc, preparatory trial, first public interrogation, Wednesday, February 21, 1431, in *The Trial of Jeanne D'Arc: Translated into English from the Original Latin and French Documents*, by W. P. Barrett (New York: Gotham House, 1932), 37–38. Content in the public domain was accessed online in Medieval Sourcebook: The Trial of Joan of Arc, https://sourcebooks.fordham.edu/basis/joanofarc-trial.asp.

Joan was raised near the border of the duchies of Bar and Lorraine. While today these areas are part of France, in the early fifteenth century they were among the many autonomous or foreign-held regions.

DAY 2

Joan of Arc, preparatory trial, second public interrogation, Thursday, February 22, 1431, in Barrett, *Trial of Jeanne D'Arc*, 42–43.

Elsewhere, Joan states that she was "in her thirteenth year," that is, twelve years of age. Most scholars believe the voices first came to her during the summer of 1424.

DAY 3

Joan of Arc, preparatory trial, fourth public interrogation, Tuesday, February 27, 1431, in Barrett, *Trial of Jeanne D'Arc*, 58, 59.

When Joan first met the future king Charles VII at Chinon, she told him she had been sent to him by God. Cautious of such claims, he sent her to Poitiers to be examined by numerous clerics. She was questioned over a period of nearly a month. Cleared by them of any heresy or falsehood, she was then given command of Charles's men. Sadly, the records of this investigation have been lost.

DAY 4

Joan of Arc, preparatory trial, second public interrogation, Thursday, February 22, 1431, in Barrett, *Trial of Jeanne D'Arc*, 43.

DAY 5

Joan of Arc, preparatory trial, private interrogation, Monday, March 12, 1431, in Barrett, *Trial of Jeanne D'Arc*, 97.

The region of Burgundy was an ally of England in the Hundred Years' War. The Burgundians captured Joan in May 1430 and handed her over to the English.

DAY 6

Jean de Metz, Joan's closest officer, testimony in Domrémy on January 31, 1456, in *Jeanne d'Arc, Maid of Orleans, Deliverer of France: Being the Story of Her Life, Her Achievements, and Her Death as Attested on Oath and Set Forth in the Original Documents*, ed. T. Douglas Murray (London: William Heinemann, 1902), 224. Content in the public domain was accessed online at Project Gutenberg, https://www.gutenberg.org/files/57389/57389-h/57389-h.htm#Page_332.

DAY 7

Catherine Leroyer, of Vaucouleurs, testimony in Domrémy on January 31, 1456, in Murray, *Jeanne d'Arc*, 227. Marie Robine (also known as Marie d'Avignon), a peasant woman who had a reputation as a prophet and visionary, had made this prediction years earlier before her death in 1399. The French title *dauphin* was reserved for the prince who was heir to the throne.

Henri Leroyer, of Vaucouleurs, testimony in Domrémy on January 31, 1456, in Murray, *Jeanne d'Arc*, 228.

DAY 8

Seguin Seguin, Dominican friar and theology professor who examined Joan at Poitiers, testimony on May 14, 1456, in Murray, *Jeanne d'Arc*, 307.

DAY 9

Joan of Arc, preparatory trial, fourth public interrogation, Tuesday, February 27, 1431, in Barrett, *Trial of Jeanne D'Arc*, 62.

Joan was illiterate, though she was able to sign her name and dictated numerous letters using assistants to write them down.

DAY 10

Simon Charles, president of the Chamber of Accounts, testimony in Paris on May 7, 1456, in *Joan of Arc: La Pucelle*, ed. and trans. Craig Taylor, Manchester Medieval Sources Series (Manchester, UK: Manchester University Press, 2006), 318; Simon Charles, president of the Chamber of Accounts, testimony in Paris on May 7, 1456, in Murray, *Jeanne d'Arc*, 291–92.

DAY 11

Jean II, Duke of Alençon, testimony on May 31, 1456, in Murray, *Jeanne d'Arc*, 280.

Joan of Arc, letter to the king of England, March 22, 1429, excerpts, in Taylor, *Joan of Arc*, 74–75.

Joan referred to herself as Joan the Maid, *La Pucelle* in French. This term implied her vow to maintain her virginity as long as God would ask her to do so.

DAY 12

Joan of Arc, preparatory trial, fourth public interrogation, Tuesday, February 27, 1431, in Barrett, *Trial of Jeanne D'Arc*, 63; Joan of Arc, preparatory trial, fourth public interrogation, Tuesday, February 27, 1431, in Murray, *Jeanne d'Arc*, 31.

DAY 13

Simon Beaucroix, squire, testimony in Paris on April 20, 1456, in Murray, *Jeanne d'Arc*, 268–69.

Jean Barbin, doctor of law, king's advocate, testimony in Paris on April 30, 1456, in Murray, *Jeanne d'Arc*, 270.

DAY 14

Jean II, Duke of Alençon, testimony in Paris on May 31, 1456, in Murray, *Jeanne d'Arc*, 278.

DAY 15

Jean, Count of Dunois, known as the Bastard of Orléans, military captain, testimony in Orléans on February 22, 1456, in Murray, *Jeanne d'Arc*, 236.

DAY 16

Jean Pasquerel, Order of the Hermit Friars of St. Augustine, Joan's confessor, testimony in Paris on May 4, 1456, in Murray, *Jeanne d'Arc*, 286.

DAY 17

Jean, Count of Dunois, known as the Bastard of Orléans, military captain, testimony on February 22, 1456, in Murray, *Jeanne d'Arc*, 234.

DAY 18

Thibauld d'Armagnac, knight and bailiff of Chartres, testimony in Paris 1455–1456, in Murray, *Jeanne d'Arc*, 294.

Jean II, Duke of Alençon, testimony on May 31, 1456, in Murray, *Jeanne d'Arc*, 281.

DAY 19

Marguerite La Touroulde, Joan's hostess, testimony in Paris in 1456, in Murray, *Jeanne d'Arc*, 271–72.

DAY 20

Jean, Count of Dunois, known as the Bastard of Orléans, military captain, testimony in Orléans on February 22, 1456, in Murray, *Jeanne d'Arc*, 239.

DAY 21

Jean, Count of Dunois, known as the Bastard of Orléans, military captain, testimony in Orléans on February 22, 1456, in Murray, *Jeanne d'Arc*, 240.

Shouting "Noel" or "Christmas" at the coronations of French kings is a tradition that began with Charlemagne because he was crowned on Christmas Day in the year 800.

DAY 22

Raimond de Macy, knight, testimony in Paris on May 12, 1456, in Murray, *Jeanne d'Arc*, 295.

Joan was captured by Burgundian forces allied with the English on May 24, 1430. She was subsequently sold to the English for a large sum. Joan's trial was paid for by the English and conducted by Pierre Cauchon, an English partisan and the bishop of Beauvais. When she was vindicated in 1456, he was posthumously excommunicated;

his remains were exhumed from the cathedral in Lisieux and thrown into a sewer.

Guillaume Manchon, notary at Joan's trial, second inquiry, testimony on May 2, 1452, in Murray, *Jeanne d'Arc*, 178–79.

DAY 23

Guillaume Manchon, notary at Joan's trial, first inquiry, testimony on March 5, 1449, in Murray, *Jeanne d'Arc*, 167–68.

Isambart de la Pierre, Dominican friar and one of Joan's interrogators, testimony in May 1456, in *The Retrial of Joan of Arc: The Evidence for Her Vindication*, by Régine Pernoud (San Francisco: Ignatius Press, 2007), 201.

DAY 24

Joan of Arc, preparatory trial, private interrogation, Saturday, March 17, 1429, in Barrett, *Trial of Jeanne D'Arc*, 125.

DAY 25

Joan of Arc, preparatory trial, third public interrogation, Saturday, February 24, 1431, in Barrett, *Trial of Jeanne D'Arc*, 51–52.

DAY 26

Joan of Arc, preparatory trial, third public interrogation, Saturday, February 24, 1431, in Barrett, *Trial of Jeanne D'Arc*, 49–50.

Jean Massieu, usher who brought Joan to her execution, second inquiry, testimony on May 8, 1452, in Murray, *Jeanne d'Arc*, 203.

DAY 27

Joan of Arc, private interrogation, preparatory trial, Wednesday, March 14, 1431, in Barrett, *Trial of Jeanne D'Arc*, 114.

DAY 28

Joan of Arc, private admonition of the maid, Wednesday, April 18, 1431, in Barrett, *Trial of Jeanne D'Arc*, 287.

DAY 29

Jean Massieu, usher who brought Joan to her execution, testimony on May 12, 1456, in Murray, *Jeanne d'Arc*, 176.

Martin Ladvenu, Dominican priest who heard Joan's last confession and accompanied her to her execution, fourth examination, testimony on May 13, 1456, in Murray, *Jeanne d'Arc*, 195.

DAY 30

Jean Ricquier, cathedral chaplain in Rouen, testimony in Rouen in May 1456, in Murray, *Jeanne d'Arc*, 302.

Isambart de la Pierre, Dominican friar and one of Joan's interrogators, third examination, testimony on May 9, 1452, in Murray, *Jeanne d'Arc*, 191.

Guillaume Manchon, notary at Joan's trial, first inquiry, testimony on March 5, 1449, in Murray, *Jeanne d'Arc*, 170.

Jaymie Stuart Wolfe is a freelance writer and editor at One More Basket, a biweekly columnist at TheBostonPilot.com, and a bimonthly columnist at OSV News. She has written numerous books for both adults and children.

Wolfe serves on the board of the Joan of Arc Project, which celebrates St. Joan of Arc year-round. The project organizes an annual street parade on January 6 that retells St. Joan of Arc's life with pageantry and draws tens of thousands.

Wolfe holds a bachelor's degree in government from Harvard University and a master's degree in ministry from St. John's Seminary in Boston.

She and her husband, Andrew, have eight children and live in New Orleans, Louisiana.